Complete Warm Routine for Classical Guitar

by Gohar Vardanyan

1   2

Visit us on the Web at www.melbay.com — E-mail us at email@melbay.com

Table of Contents

Introduction

This book is intended for guitarists who are looking for a concise warm-up routine that does not involve learning too many different and complicated exercises. In the last twenty plus years of playing the guitar, I have gone through many different warm-up routines and found that I always come back to these basic exercises, while forgetting most others. These exercises can be used to fit individual needs in terms of availability of warm-up time and general skill level. At a slower tempo they are simple enough for beginners, but can be made more challenging by increasing the speed, for example, or barring with the first finger when playing the scales and the slurs.

With the exception of one etude that is used as the basis for a variety of arpeggio and tremolo exercises, every other exercise is a simple, short scale or pattern that is repeated on different strings and in different positions. This eliminates the need to learn any extra repertoire and leaves our minds free for pieces we actually want to play.

The book is divided into four sections:
  I: Arpeggios
  II: Scales
  III: Tremolo
  IV: Slurs

Each section has a short paragraph explaining the exercise and "General Instructions" on how to practice it. There is enough material to spend an hour on just warm-up. However, not all of these exercises need to be played in one day or in one practice session. If short on time, you can pick and choose which to practice on that day. It is best to do at least five minutes from each category - arpeggio, scales, tremolo, slurs – each day. I usually like to keep that specific category order. If time is no issue, these exercises can not only act as a short warm-up, but also to advance and improve technique by doing all the variations, paying close attention to accuracy and clarity, and gradually increasing the tempo.

The exercises should be practiced with a metronome, beginning with a slow tempo and gradually increasing it as the hands warm up. When trying to build up the tempo, slow and steady is best, but sometimes you will need to push yourself just beyond your comfort zone, to see what is possible. One of the ways to push yourself is to move the metronome speed two notches up, then one notch back, two forward, one back, etc… This method gives a little push, and then relaxes, while still moving forward.

As with anything we play, pay constant attention to how the hands feel. If there is any tension or fatigue, it is best to take a break, relax and come back to it later. The "no pain, no gain" method does not work for having relaxed technique and staying injury free.

I: ARPEGGIOS

It is best to start any warm up with a set of arpeggios using a combination of free stroke and rest stroke with the *a* finger. A full sextuplet arpeggio, like the one below, allows for a gradual warm-up while saving time by involving all four right hand fingers at once. The following etude by Mauro Giuliani has fairly simple left hand chords, so concentration can be on the right hand sextuplet arpeggio *p-i-m-a-m-i*.

General Instructions:
* The etude should be played with the *a* finger both free-stroke as well as rest-stroke.
* Metronome settings should be varied to accommodate subdivisions of 2 notes per beat, 3 notes per beat, and ultimately, 6 notes per beat.
* Attention should be paid to the evenness of the arpeggio, both in time, i.e. rhythm, and in volume.

Etude No. 5, Op. 48

Mauro Giuliani

The same etude can now be turned into a different exercise by reversing the right hand pattern to *p-a-m-i-m-a*. This new pattern creates a different challenge for the right hand by doubling the *a* finger. After playing in reverse, the regular pattern becomes much easier.

Though not required, the *a* finger can be played with rest stroke in this pattern as well. It will be more challenging, since *a* has to play twice, right before and after *p*. The rest of the General Instructions above also apply.

Etude No. 5, Op. 48

Mauro Giuliani

Arpeggio Exercise: 6 String *p a m i*

The following is a full 6-strings repeating arpeggio pattern. Here it is written on simple chords, as a short right hand warm up. However, for more variety it can be used on any etude that uses all 6 strings, e.g. Etude no. 1 by Villa Lobos.

General Instructions:
- Play the *a* finger with both rest stroke as well as free stroke.
- All ascending 3-note groups are played with *p-i-m*
- All descending 3-note groups are played with *a-m-i*

II: SCALES

Next step in the warm up is scales. There are all sorts of different scales that can be used for a warm up. For the purpose of this book, a regular one position, two-octave, G major scale will be used, then shifted chromatically up to D major, or until the 4th finger reaches the 12th fret. It is better to use a simple scale, that has no open strings and uses all six strings, in order to be able to move up the fret board and freely do all the rhythmic variations. The following scales and exercises are meant for rest stroke, but can also be played free stroke, depending on individual needs and area of improvement.

General Instructions:
- All of the following scales should be practiced with *i-m-i-m, m-i-m-i,* as well as *m-a-m-a,* and *a-m-a-m.* *Beginning with *m,* while playing with *m-i,* will reverse cross string shifts in the right hand, thus making it more challenging. Same applies if beginning with *a,* while playing with *a-m.*

- Metronome setting should be varied to accommodate subdivisions of 2 notes per beat, 3 notes per beat, and ultimately 4 and 6 notes per beat.

- All ascending chromatic shifts are provided below, with only two complete descending shifts. When practicing, continue shifting chromatically downwards to reach G major, or F♯ major by shifting one extra time.

- The scales should be played consecutively, without stopping, to increase stamina.

- There are no shifts within the scales, only when moving to the next one.

- To increase difficulty, the left hand can hold down a bar with the first finger while the other fingers play the scale.

Scales

It is important to also practice different rhythmic variations of the scale to increase the accuracy and speed. All of the above "General Instructions" apply to these variations as well. Only the first scale of the sequence is provided. When practicing, ascend chromatically up to D-major, just like in the previous exercise; then descend back to G major.

Exercises 1 and 2 are just simple dotted rhythms, exercises 3-7 are speed bursts of different lengths, starting with 3-note bursts, then 4-note, 5-note, etc… These give the fingers a chance to play a set of notes very quickly, then have a short break before playing the next set. The longer the speed burst, the more difficult it is. A less advanced player can choose not to play the longer bursts. All bursts start on the beat. For notation's sake, the bursts are written to fit into 4/4 meter; however, they should be played as fast as possible, while keeping clarity and accuracy. For example, in Exercise 3, the 32nd notes will be faster than their metronomic value and the dotted 8th note will be longer; same with the triplets in Exercise 4, and so on. Ultimately, the metronome setting should remain the same for all sets of bursts, the longer the bursts, the faster it will be to fit in the same beat duration.

Exercise 1: Dotted 8th and 16th

Exercise 2: 16th and dotted 8th

Exercise 3: 3-note bursts

Exercise 4: 4-note bursts

Exercise 5: 5-note bursts

Exercise 6: 6-note bursts

Exercise 7: 7-note bursts

Chromatic Patterns

General Instructions:

- All of the following exercises should be practiced with *i-m-i-m*, *m-i-m-i*, as well as *m-a-m-a* and *a-m-a-m*.
- 8th notes are to be played staccato, which allows for the next finger to prepare for the next note. 16th notes are legato.
- The example below is given in first position. Shift one fret up and repeat the exercise, until 4th finger reaches the 12th fret.

Exercise 1: 4 Note Chromatic (no open string)

The next exercise goes two notes forward, then one back, two forward again. This can also be practiced in bursts, like the non-chromatic scale exercises before. Variation can be created by going three notes forward, two back, three notes forward again, etc…Because of the use of the open string, this scale cannot be shifted in position and is meant to be played in first position only. Note: For the switch between the 3rd and 2nd strings, the note B can be played either on the open 2nd string, or on the 4th fret of the 3rd string.

Exercise 2: Continuous Chromatic

III: TREMOLO

Tremolo is one of those techniques that require constant maintenance. It is important to keep up with it in a warm-up, even if there are no tremolo pieces in the current repertoire. The below exercise is the same Etude no. 5 by Mauro Giuliani that was used in the arpeggio section in the beginning of the book. However, instead of the arpeggio, the right hand will be playing the tremolo pattern on the first string and the thumb will be filling in the rest of the notes in the chord. The more the thumb jumps around the strings the more difficult it will be to control the evenness of the tremolo. The excerpt after the main exercise has the thumb playing a more consecutive bass pattern by inverting the order of the bass notes, thus allowing for an easier control of tremolo evenness.

General Instructions:
- Aside from the regular *p-a-m-i* tremolo pattern, *p-a-m-a, p-m-a-m, p-m-i-m, p-i-m-i,* and *p-i-m-a* should also be practiced. These help with finger independence, which ultimately makes the regular tremolo easier and more even.
- Metronome settings must vary to play 4 notes per beat, i.e. the beat falls only on *p,* as well as 2 notes per beat, i.e. beat falls on *p* and on *m.*

- As an extra challenge, when playing 4 notes per beat, the metronome beat can be changed to fall on any of the other fingers, instead of *p,* thus off-setting the beginning of the pattern. E.g. instead of playing ***p**-a-m-i-**p**-a-m-i*, play: ***i**-p-a-m-**i**-p-a-m* or ***m**-i-p-a-**m**-i-p-a* or ***a**-m-i-p-**a**-m-i-p*, etc… *bold signifies metronome beat.

Etude No. 5 - Modified for Tremolo

Mauro Giuliani

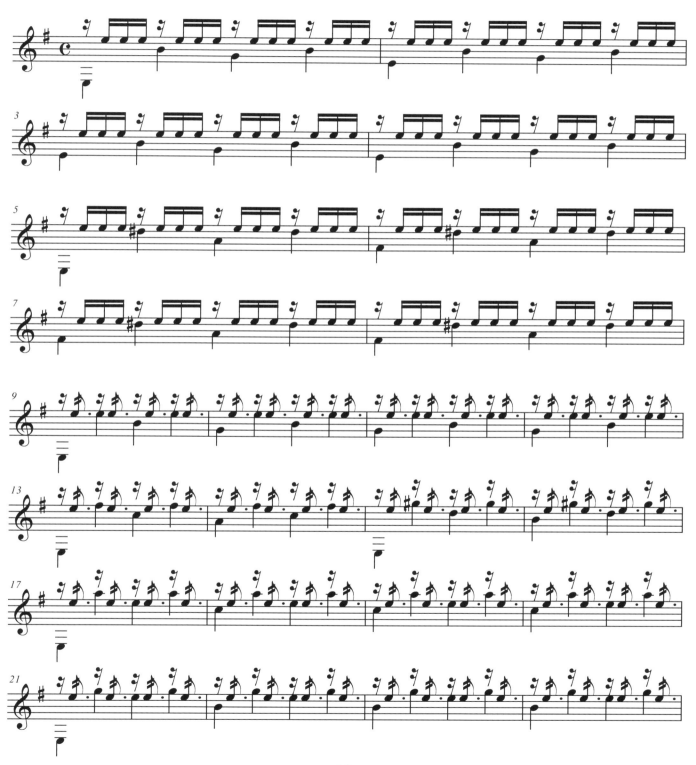

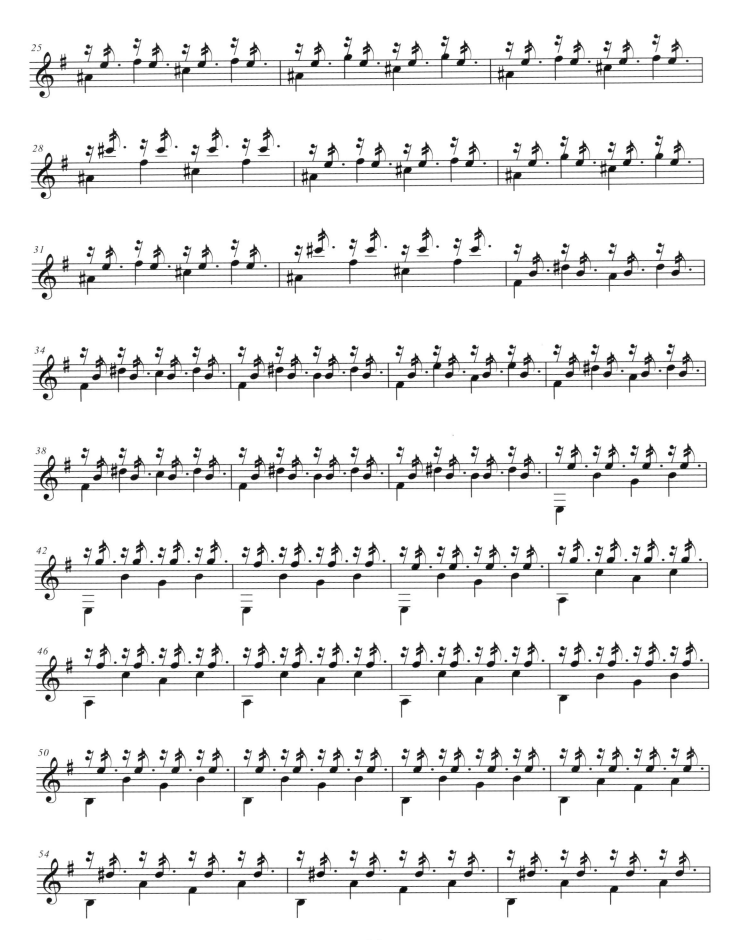

Optional Consecutive Bass Pattern:

IV: SLURS

Slurs are an important part of the left hand warm-up, as well as a technical exercise. The exercises below are a combination of pull-offs and hammer-ons to cover both techniques at the same time and save time. These exercises start on the 6th string, go down to 1st and come back to 6th. For variety, they can be reversed, to start on the 1st string, go up to the 6th string, back to 1st and so on. One complete set is written out. The exercises can be continued up the fret board until the 4th finger reaches the 12th fret. Or, as in the case of the Triplets, also down the fret board to 1st position. The "Triplets" exercise begins in 5th position because it is actually easier to play it in the middle of the fret board than in 1st position.

General Instructions:
- Keep general rhythmic evenness between the played and the slurred notes.
- Keep fingers close to the fret board when hammering on or pulling off.
- Keep fingers not playing the slur on the strings.
- The slurs should be played consecutively, without stopping, to increase stamina.
- To increase difficulty, the left hand can hold down a bar with the first finger, while the other fingers play the slurs.

Exercise 1: Duplets

16

Exercise 2: Triplets

Gohar Vardanyan
Classical Guitar

Web: www.goharvardanyan.com • *E-mail:* goharvardanyan@gmail.com

BIOGRAPHY

Armenian guitarist Gohar Vardanyan has performed throughout the United States for numerous guitar societies, universities, and arts organizations, including the Smithsonian Institution in Washington, DC, Alice Tully Hall at Lincoln Center, and the Grand Canyon, Sierra Nevada, South Bay, Great Lakes and New England Guitar Societies. She has appeared on National Public Radio in the United Stated on the program "From the Top" and Radio Nacional in Argentina. Ms. Vardanyan has performed with the Juilliard Opera Center and as a soloist with the Great Lakes Chamber Orchestra and Panama National Symphony Orchestra. She has also been a guest artist at the "Encuentro Internacional de Guitarra" in Panama and the Hamilton International Guitar Festival in Canada. Guitar International Magazine has described her as "the complete package," "with a musicality and emotional quality . . . that one would expect from someone much older than the young wunderkind. Not only is she able to draw you into her performances with engaging musical interpretations, but she has the technical facility that is required of any concert level guitarist." Her playing has been described as "passionate," "evocative," and "virtuosic."

In addition to her performing career, Ms. Vardanyan is an avid teacher. She has taught in master classes for various universities, guitar societies, and festivals in the United States as well as abroad. While still at Juilliard, she was a recipient of two teaching fellowships. She has taught music classes through the Morse Fellowship and group guitar classes through the Instrumental Music Program in New York City's public schools. She was also a recipient of the McCabe Guitar Fellowship for interactive performances for NYC's public school students.

Ms. Vardanyan began studying the guitar in her native Armenia at the age of five under the careful guidance of her father, Vardan Vardanyan. At the age of eight, she gave her first public performance and also appeared on Armenian National Television. She was the first prize winner in the Armenian National Music Contest "Amadeus" and was accepted into the prestigious group, "New Names," for talented young musicians. She performed in numerous concert venues in Armenia, including Komitas Chamber Music Hall and the Small Philharmonic Hall. She went on to study with Antigoni Goni at the Pre-College Division of the Juilliard School. In 2001, Ms. Vardanyan studied with John Wunsch at the Interlochen Arts Academy. She was awarded the Young Artist's Certificate from Interlochen Center for the Arts and the Harold Randolph Prize in performance from the Peabody Conservatory.

Ms. Vardanyan holds a Master of Music Degree from The Juilliard School where she studied with Sharon Isbin, and a Bachelor of Music degree from the Peabody Conservatory of Music where she studied with Manuel Barrueco. She is also an alumna of the Aspen Music Festival and School.

Notes

WWW.MELBAY.COM

Printed in Great Britain
by Amazon